Introducing The Positions...

for VIOLIN—Vol. II
SECOND, FOURTH, SIXTH AND SEVENTH POSITIONS

INTRODUCING THE POSITIONS, Volume Two, is a continuation of the course of study started in INTRODUCING THE POSITIONS, Volume One. In the latter work the third and fifth positions were taken up, and in the present work the second, fourth, sixth, seventh, and higher positions are introduced. It is true that violinists usually employ the third and fifth positions much more than any of the other higher positions; yet it also is true that they must become thoroughly acquainted with the second, fourth, sixth, and seventh positions. There are many passages in both solo and orchestral literature that can be played to a decided advantage by employing the second, fourth, or sixth positions. An untimely crossing of strings often is eliminated by using them, and again an undue amount of shifting sometimes is avoided. Furthermore, the works of various modern composers require that extensive use be made of these positions. As for the seventh position, it is used chiefly as a continuation of the shifting process in which the player goes from the first to the third position, and then from the third to the fifth position. The seventh, and even higher positions (eighth, ninth and tenth), are to be found in many passages of concertos and other virtuoso compositions, as well as in the works of advanced orchestral literature.

The so-called "half position," which some violinists have considered a higher position, is in reality nothing more than a substitute fingering used chiefly to eliminate clumsy fingering in the first position. It is employed only for a few measures at a time in an occasional spot in etudes, solos, and concertos, and space is not sufficient in the present work to take up this substitute fingering. When encountering passages which are simplified by use of this substitute fingering, players should have no difficulty in performing them; in fact, a study of the passages themselves, when actually encountered, will suffice for a mastery of this so-called position.

INTRODUCING THE POSITIONS, Volumes One and Two, constitute together, an introductory school of position playing. In the standard etudes of *Kayser*, *Blumenstengel*, *Mazas*, *Dont*, *Kreutzer*, *Fiorillo*, *Rode*, *Leonard*, *Dancla*, *De Beriot*, *Rovelli* and *Gavinies*, there are afforded many excellent opportunities for further study of the positions.

Harvey S. Whistler, Ph. D.

RUBANK, INC.   HAL•LEONARD®
7777 W. BLUEMOUND RD. P.O. BOX 13819 MILWAUKEE, WI 53213

The Second Position

This position is NOT to be studied until the player has completed all of the third and fifth position studies presented in "Introducing the Positions," Vol. I.

Preparatory Studies in the Key of C Major

⌐=Half-step; fingers close together

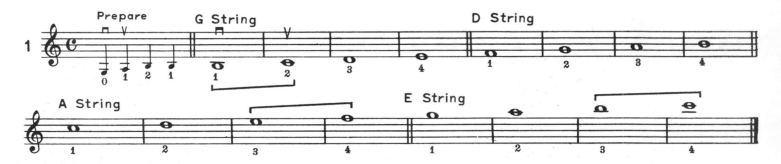

In playing positions, do not employ open E, A or D strings unless fingering is so marked.

ALARD

Copyright MCMXLVI by Rubank, Inc., Chicago, Ill
International Copyright Secured

Selected Studies in the Second Position

ALARD

De BERIOT

ALARD

De BERIOT

Exercise

Foundation Study

Etude in C

Key of F Major

Etude

Also practice (1) slurring each four tones, and (2) slurring each complete measure.

SCHOLZ

* Remain in the second position, merely stretching the first finger backward.

Key of B♭ Major

Etude

SITT

Advanced Etude in the Second Position
(Based on a Rode Caprice)

RODE

🡒 indicates an extension of the 4th finger.

Shifting from First to Second Position

When shifting from the first to a higher position, do not take the finger up and put it down again; instead, *slide* into the higher position.

Shifting from One Finger to Another

The student should shift forward on the finger that was last down, and likewise, shift backward on the finger that was last down.

The small note in the following exercises indicates the movement of the finger in shifting, and as the student perfects his ability to shift from one note to another, the small note eventually must not be heard.

E String

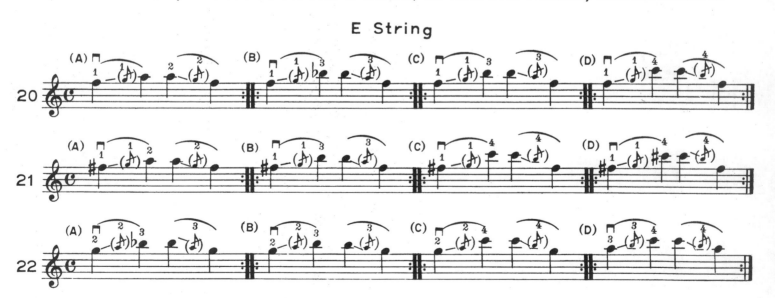

A String

D String

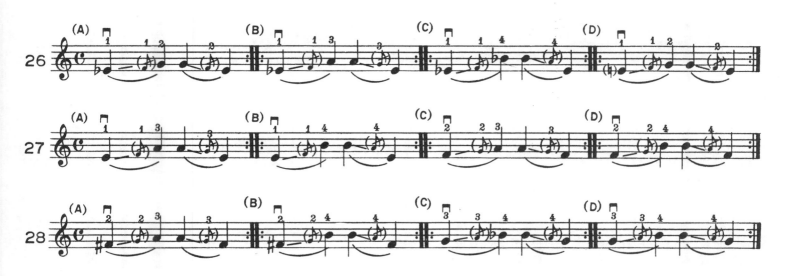

G String

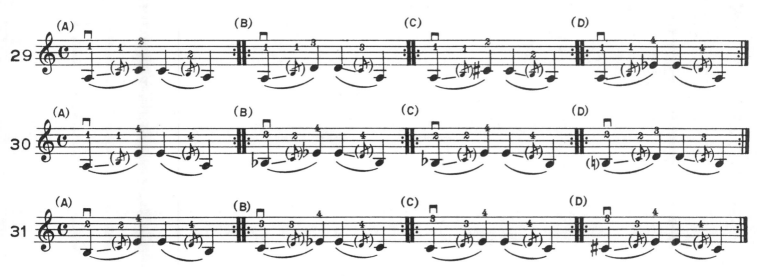

Etude in the 1st, 2nd and 3rd Positions

SITT

Also practice slowly, using a separate bow for each tone.

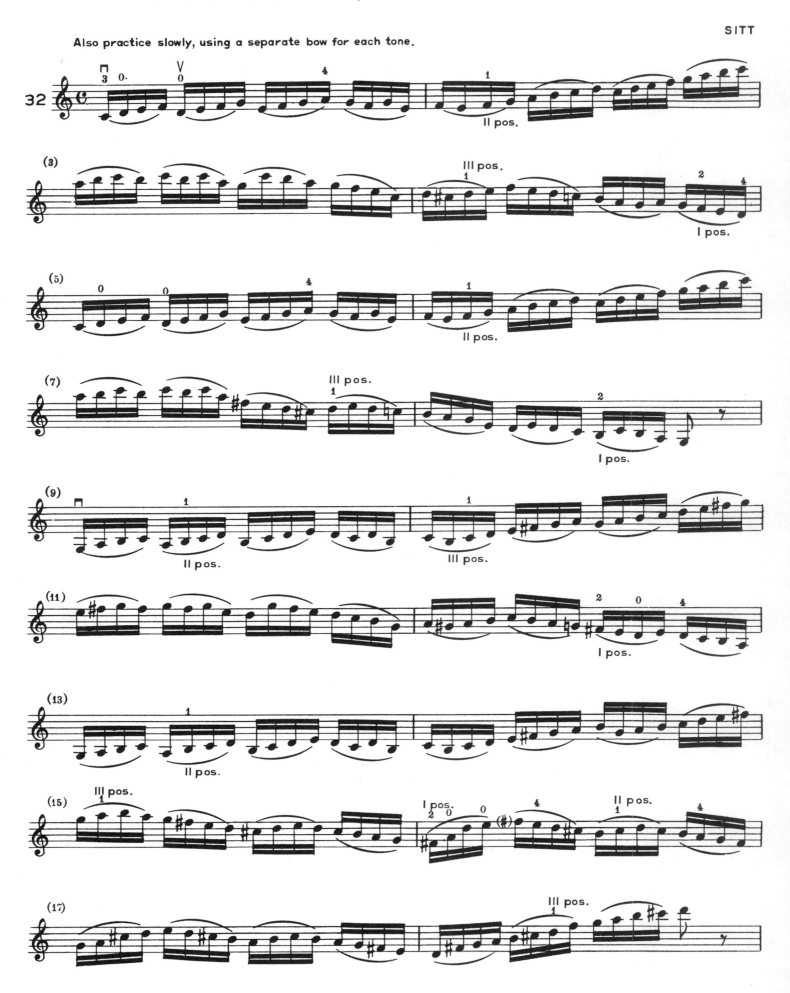

The Fourth Position
Preparatory Studies in the Key of C Major

High Tones in the Fourth Position

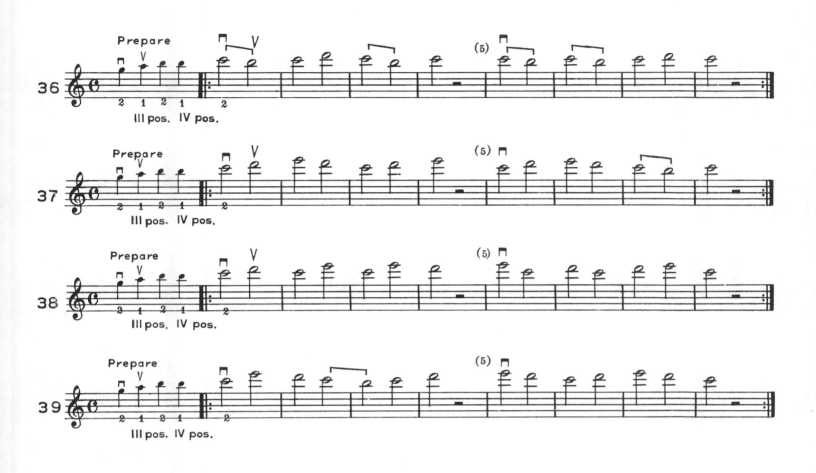

Technic Builders

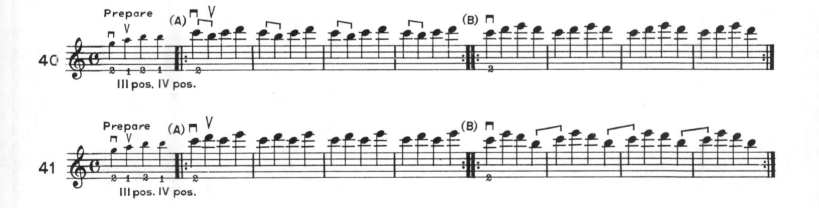

Extending the Fourth Finger

Key of F Major

Etude

DANCLA

Key of B♭ Major

Etude

RIES

Also practice slowly, using a separate bow for each tone.

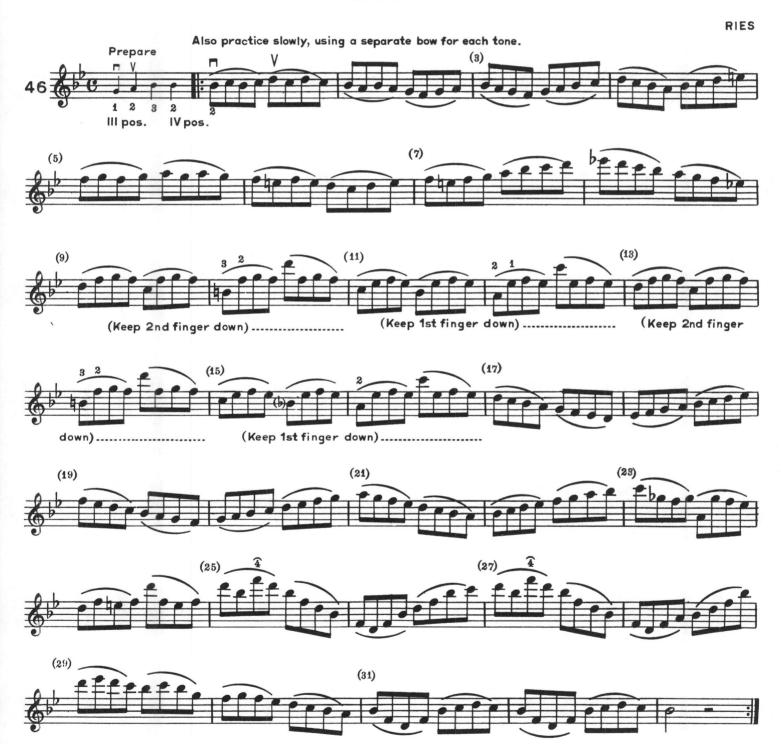

Key of G Major

Etude

RIES

Key of D Major

49

Etude

SITT

Also practice slowly, using a separate bow for each tone.

50

Shifting to the Fourth Position

The student must remember that in shifting from one position to another he is NOT to take the finger up and put it down again; instead, he is to *slide* into the higher position.

FROM THIRD TO FOURTH POSITION

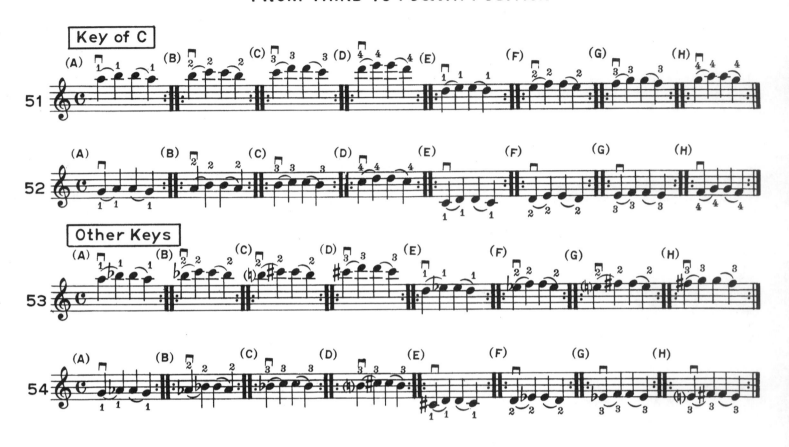

FROM SECOND TO FOURTH POSITION

Shifting from One Finger to Another

The student must remember to shift forward on the finger that was last down, and likewise to shift back-ward on the finger that was last down. The student also must remember that the small note in the following ex-ercises merely indicates the movement of the finger in shifting, and as the ability to shift from one note to another is perfected, the small note eventually must not be heard.

Etude in the Second and Fourth Positions

SCHOEN

Shifting Etude
(Through Five Positions)

Advanced Shifting Etude
(Through Five Positions)

SITT

25

The Sixth Position

At this stage of advancement, the student, in addition to taking up the Sixth Position, should turn to the *Keloeber Artist Scale and Chord Studies for the Violin*, and in a systematic fashion, study the advanced technical exercises presented in this valuable work.

Preparatory Studies in the Key of C Major

The fingering of the *sixth* position is the same as the fingering of the second position (i.e., identical notes require the same fingers), only a string lower, and at a higher place on the fingerboard.

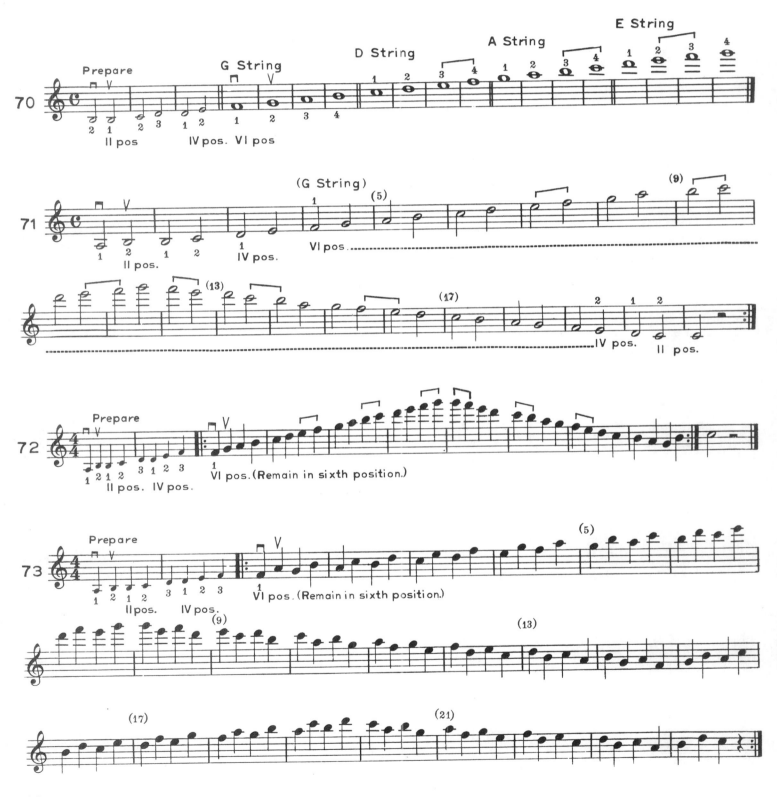

High Tones in the Sixth Position

Technic Builders

Extending the Fourth Finger

Sixth Position Etude in C

SITT

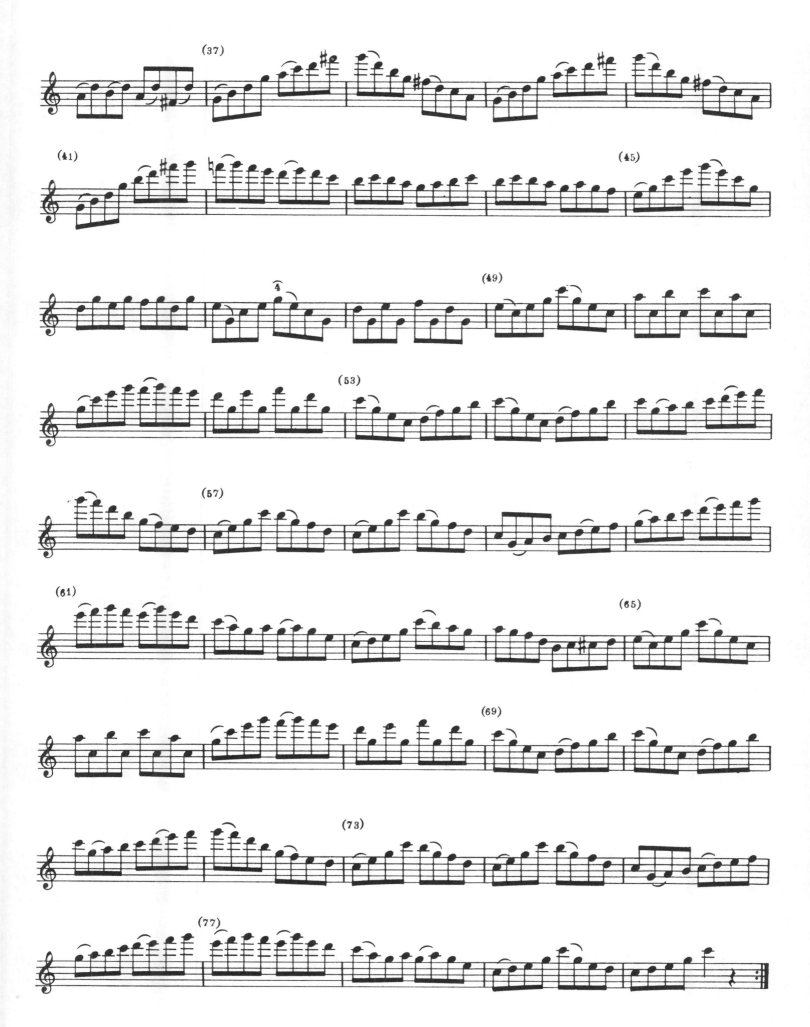

Sixth Position Etude in G

RIES

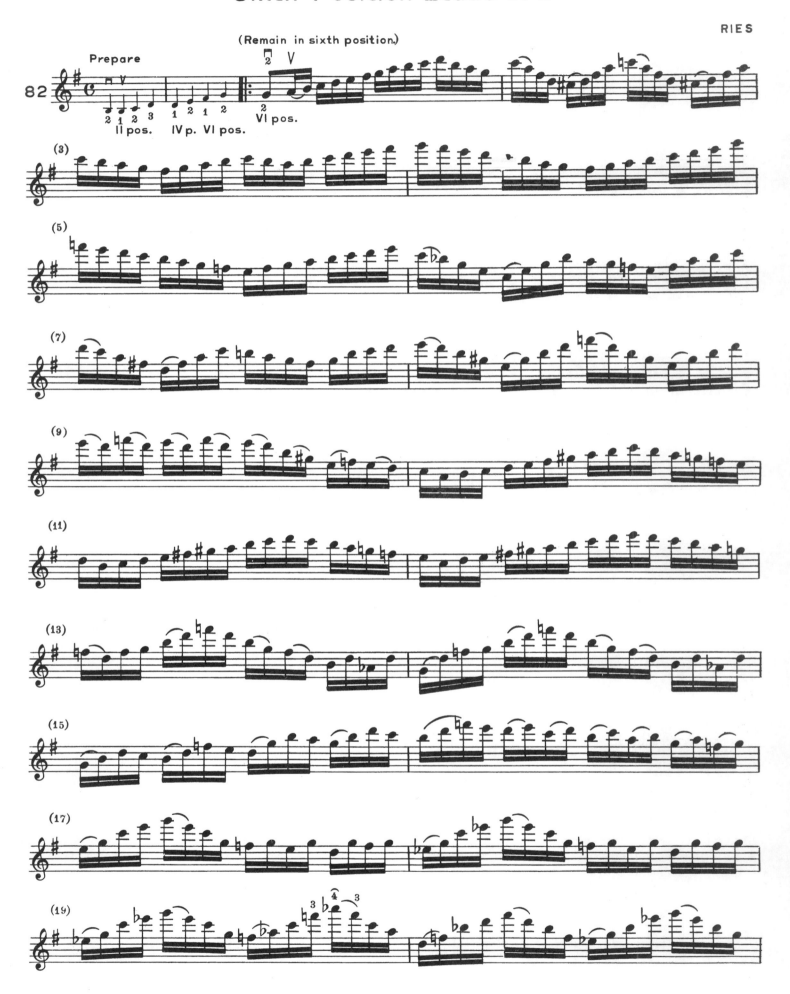

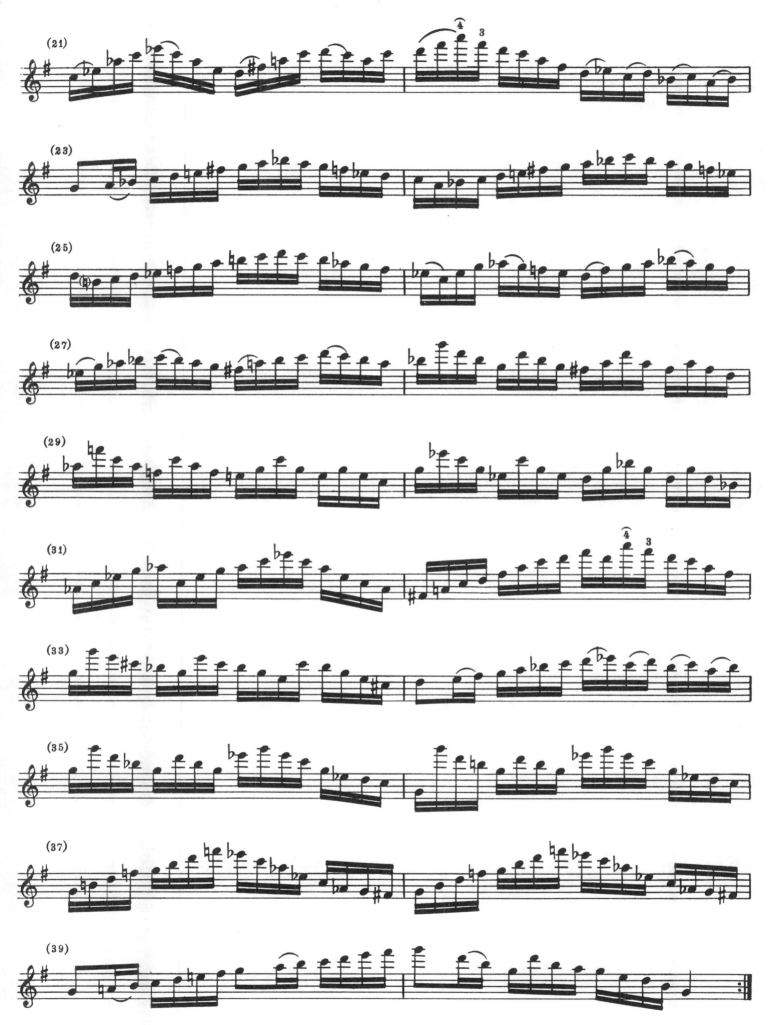

Sevcik Exercises for Shifting the Position

SECOND TO FOURTH AND FOURTH TO SIXTH POSITIONS

Scholz Exercises for Shifting the Position

SECOND TO FOURTH POSITION

FIRST TO FOURTH POSITION

FOURTH TO SIXTH POSITION

SECOND TO SIXTH POSITION

Etude Melodique
2nd, 4th and 6th Positions

De BERIOT

Also practice (1) slurring each four tones, and (2) slurring each eight tones.

Shifting Etude
(Through Six Positions)

SITT

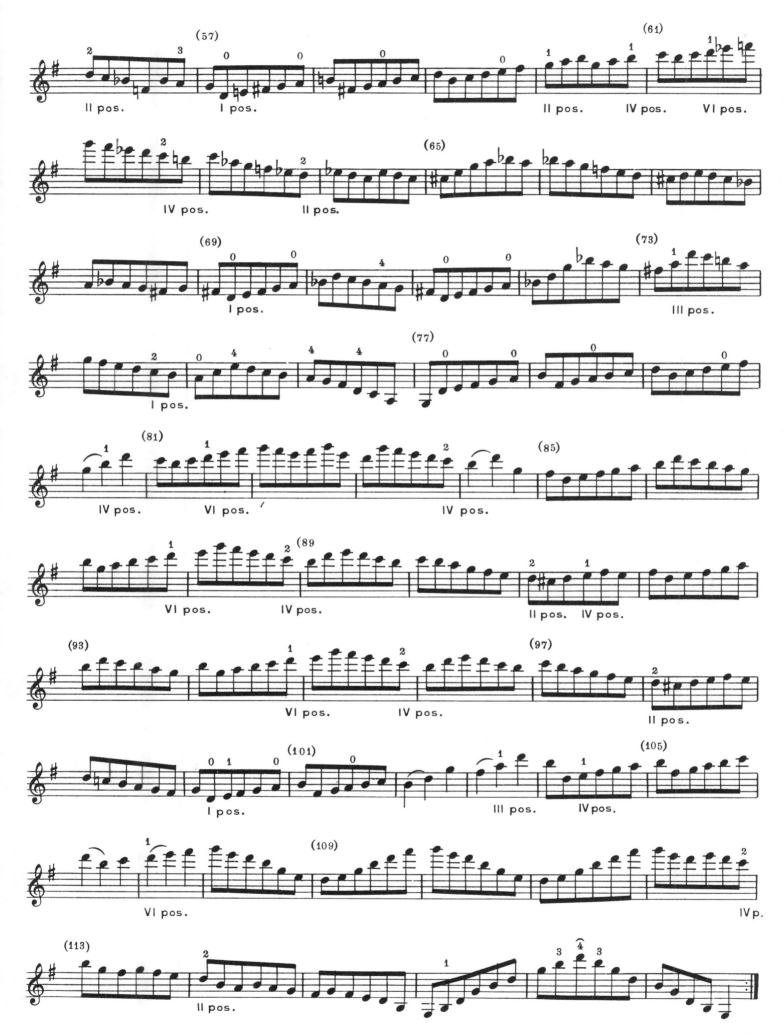

The Seventh Position
Preparatory Studies in the Key of C Major

The fingering of the *seventh* position is the same as the fingering of the third position (i.e., identical notes require the same fingers), only a string lower, and at a higher place on the fingerboard.

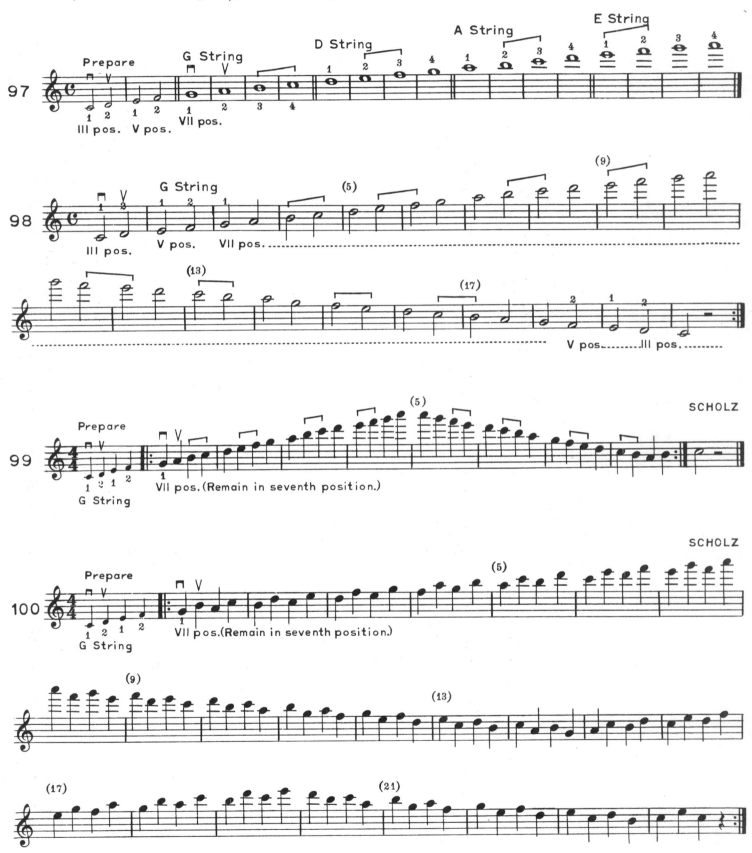

High Tones in the Seventh Position

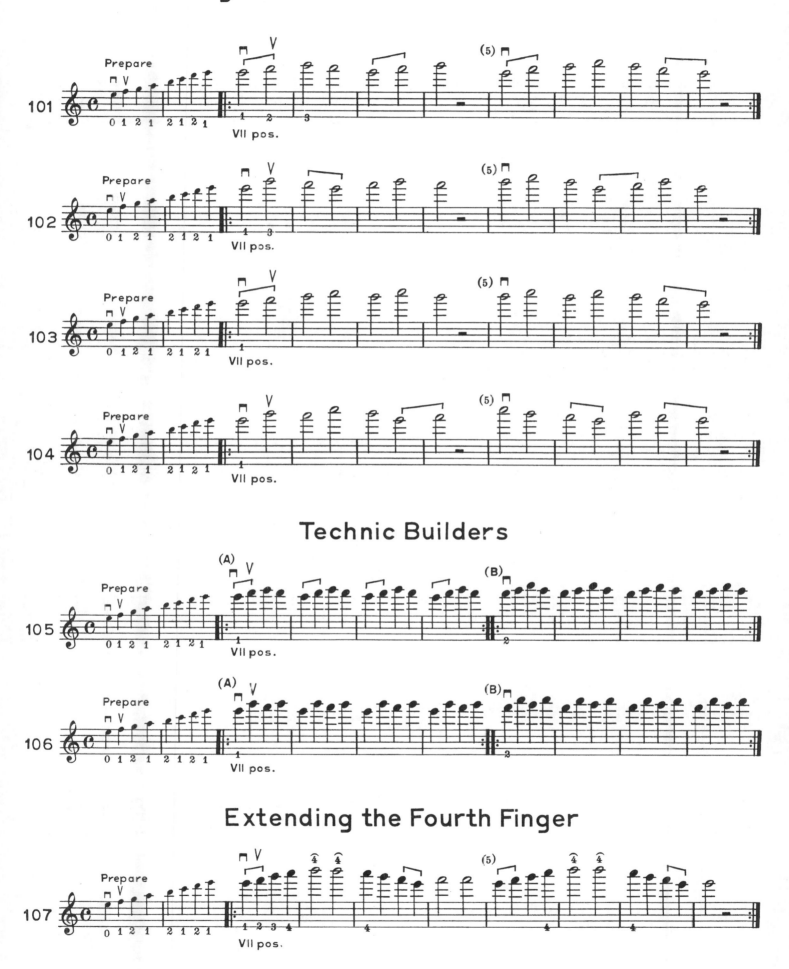

Technic Builders

Extending the Fourth Finger

Seventh Position Etude in F

SITT

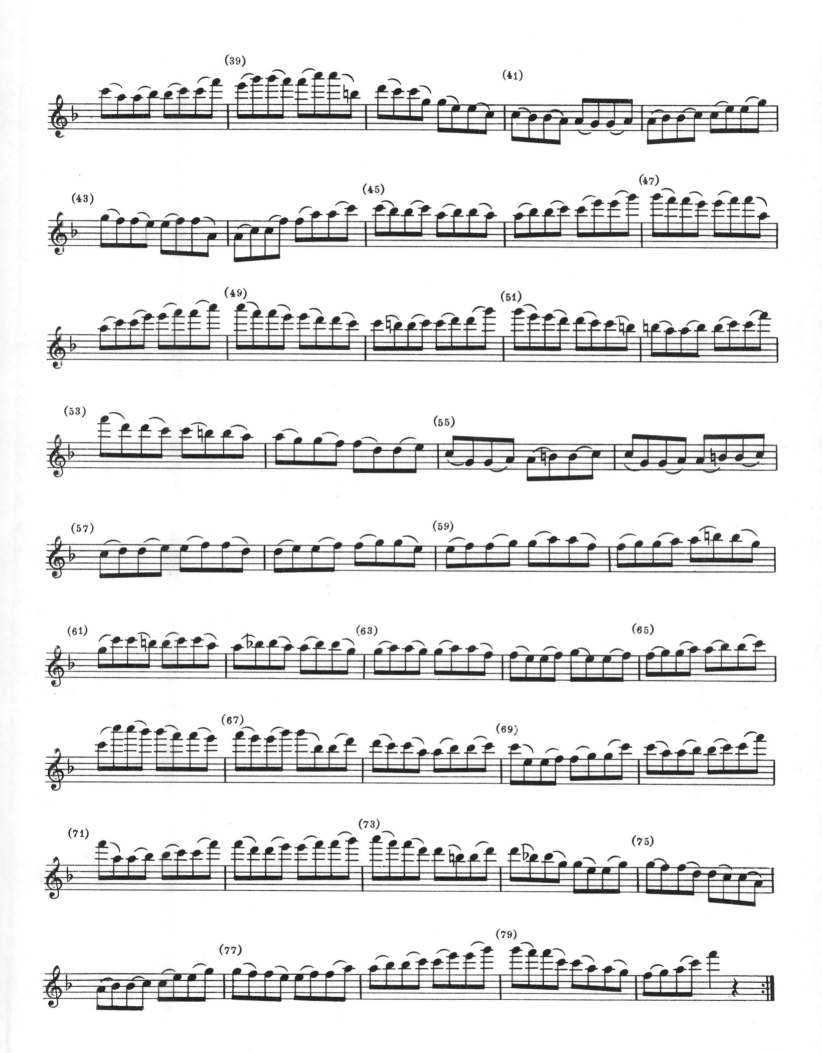

Seventh Position Etude in G

SCHOLZ

Also practice slowly, using a separate bow for each tone.

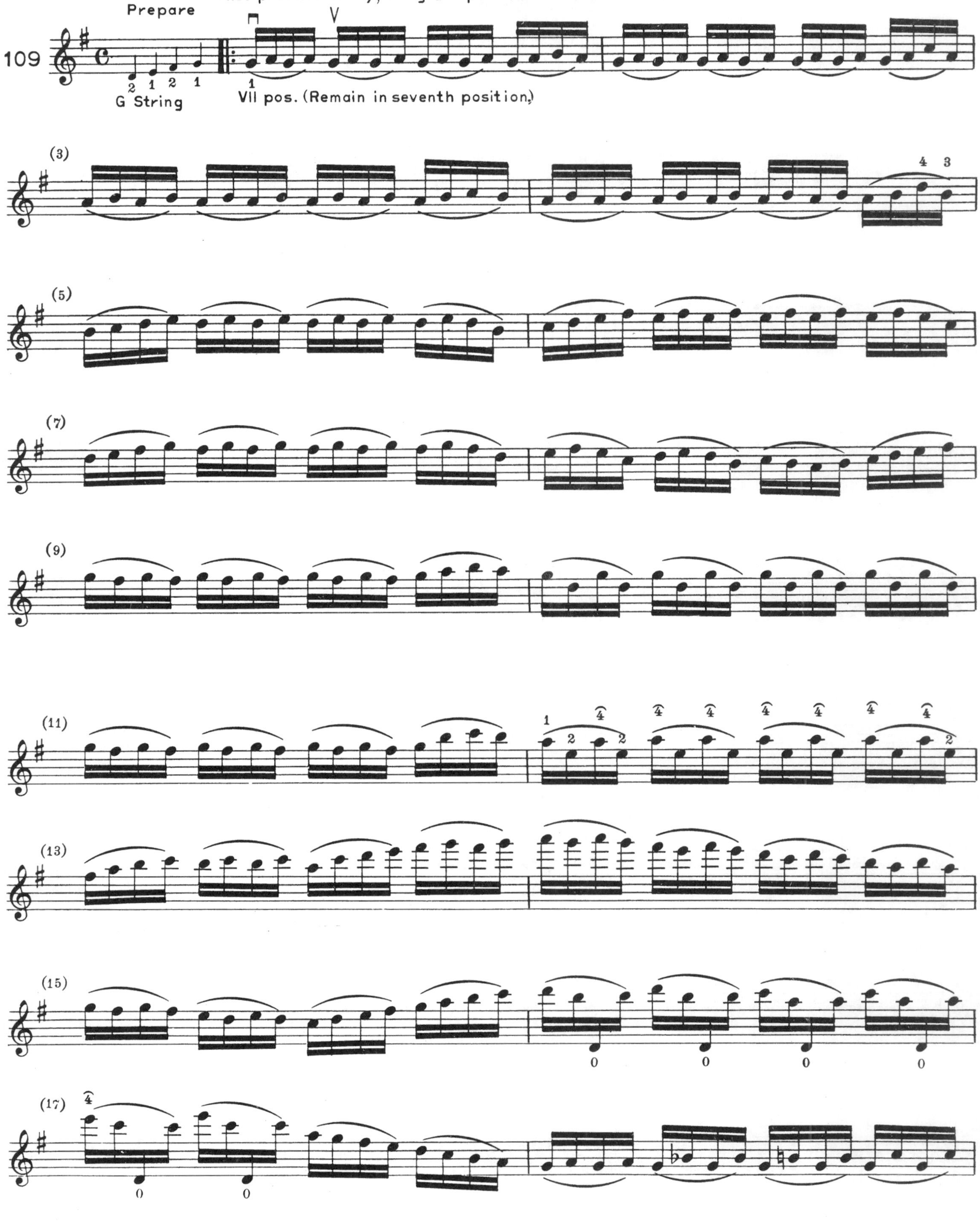

Prepare

109

G String

VII pos. (Remain in seventh position.)

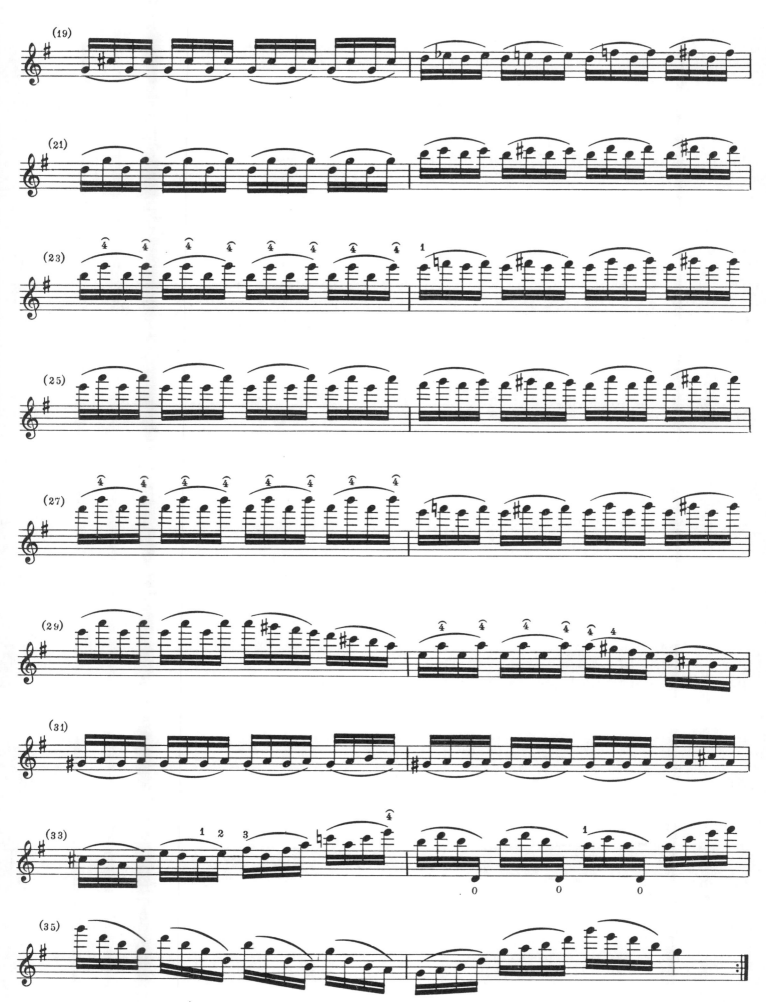

Shifting in the 3rd, 5th and 7th Positions*

G String

*As taught by the eminent Dutch violinist and graduate of the Royal Conservatorium in Amsterdam, Holland, Professor K. Bering.

A String

E String

Etude Harmonique
(3rd, 5th and 7th Positions)

De BERIOT

Also practice (1) slurring each four tones, and (2) slurring each eight tones.

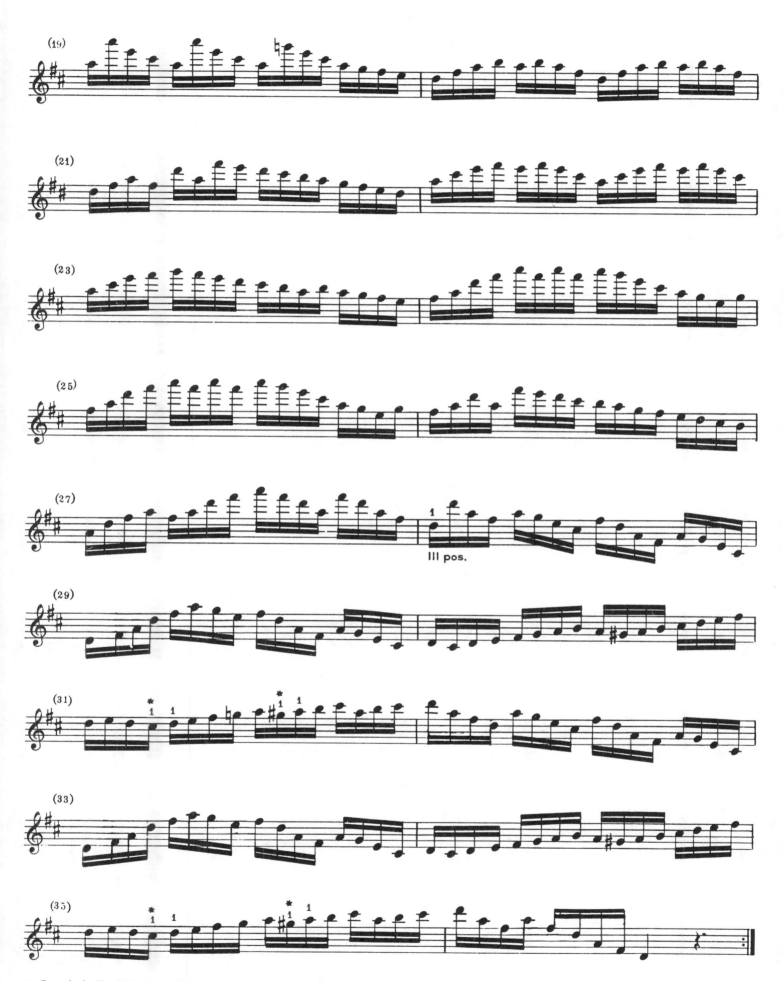

* Remain in the third position, merely stretching the first finger backward.

Shifting Etude
(Through Seven Positions)

SITT

Also practice slowly, using a separate bow for each tone.

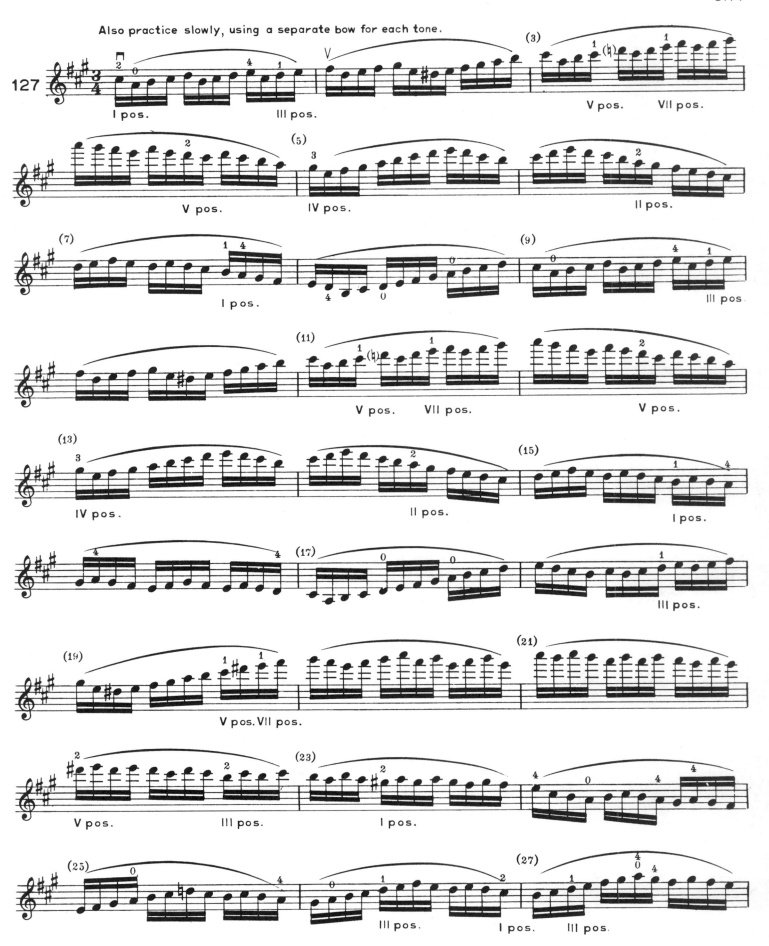

Schradieck Exercises for Shifting the Position

(Second through the Ninth Position)

SHIFTING ON THE "E" STRING

The following exercises also should be practiced in a descending manner, i. e., from the IX position back to the II position.

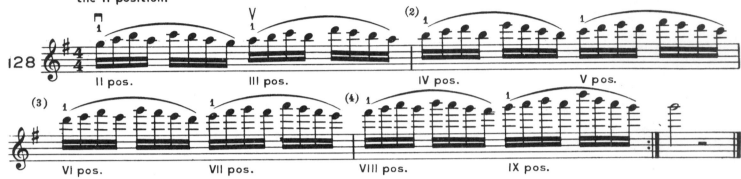

SHIFTING ON THE "A" STRING

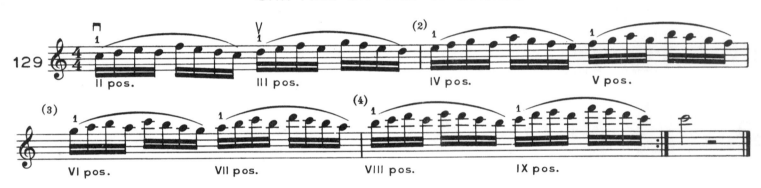

SHIFTING ON THE "D" STRING

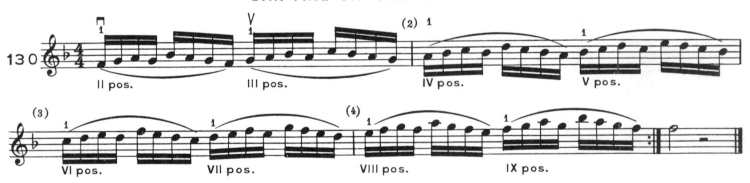

SHIFTING ON THE "G" STRING

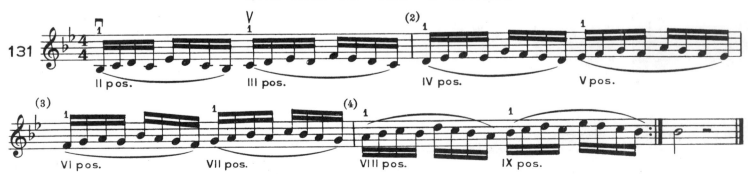

Arpeggi Through Higher Positions*

HERMANN

*Arpeggi fingerings are optional. Teachers should substitute their own fingerings when they are better suited for their needs.

Allegro de Concert

DUET

HENNING

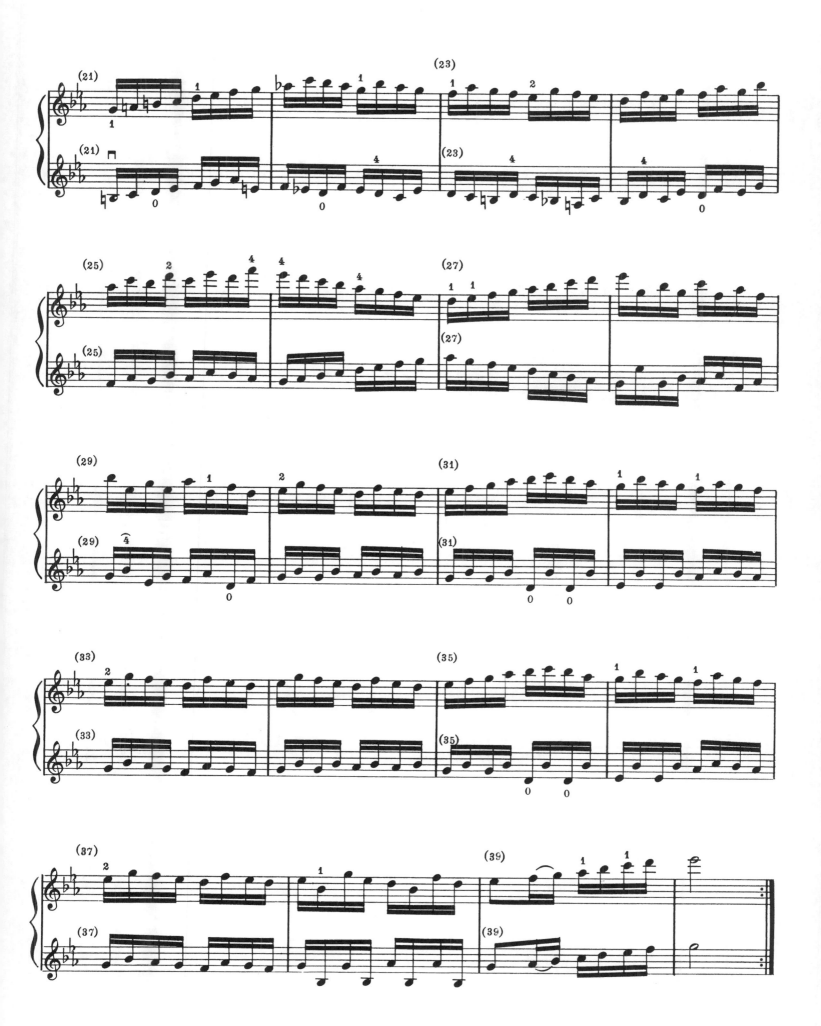

Etude Brillante
(Through Higher Positions)

De BERIOT

Also practice (1) slurring each three tones, (2) slurring each six tones, and (3) slurring each complete measure.

Etude d'Artiste
(Solo for the E String)

CAMPAGNOLI